# Composting Fun

Written by Katherine Chu

GRL Consultant, Diane Craig, Certified Literacy Specialist

Lerner Publications ◆ Minneapolis

**Note from a GRL Consultant**
This Pull Ahead leveled book has been carefully designed for beginning readers. A team of guided reading literacy experts has reviewed and leveled the book to ensure readers pull ahead and experience success.



Lerner Publications
An imprint of Lerner Publishing Group, Inc.
241 First Avenue North
Minneapolis, MN 55401 USA

For reading levels and more information, look up this title at www.lernerbooks.com.

Main body text set in Memphis Pro 24/39
Typeface provided by Linotype.

Photo Acknowledgments
The images in this book are used with the permission of: © MisterStock/Shutterstock Images, p. 3; © New Africa/Shutterstock Images, pp. 4–5; © New Africa/Adobe Stock, pp. 6–7, 16 (middle); © nieriss/Shutterstock Images, pp. 8–9; © Jurga Jot/Shutterstock Images pp. 10–11; © Kewiko/Shutterstock Images, pp. 12–13, 16 (left); © Andrea Obzerova/ Adobe Stock, pp. 14–15, 16 (right).

Front cover: © jbphotographylt/Adobe Stock

**Library of Congress Cataloging-in-Publication Data**

Names: Chu, Katherine, author.
Title: Composting fun / written by Katherine Chu.
Description: Minneapolis : Lerner Publications, [2025] | Series: In the garden (pull ahead readers – nonfiction) | Includes index. | Audience: Ages 4–7 | Audience: Grades K–1 | Summary: "Turn old plants and food scraps into nutrient rich soil for your garden! This engaging and leveled text introduces emergent readers to composting. Pairs with the fiction title Composting Pie"— Provided by publisher.
Identifiers: LCCN 2024009133 (print) | LCCN 2024009134 (ebook) | ISBN 9798765647745 (library binding) | ISBN 9798765661963 (paperback) | ISBN 9798765655399 (epub)
Subjects: LCSH: Compost—Juvenile literature.
Classification: LCC QL110.5 .C48 2025 (print) | LCC QL110.5 (ebook) | DDC 631.8/75—dc23/eng/20240415

LC record available at https://lccn.loc.gov/2024009133
LC ebook record available at https://lccn.loc.gov/2024009134

Manufactured in the United States of America
1 – CG – 12/15/24

# Table of Contents

# Composting Fun

Composting helps the Earth.

Compost is made from old food and plants.

You put the old food or plants in a bin.

Then, you mix the compost.

Next, you add water.

Compost turns into dirt. You can add the dirt to your garden.

Compost helps your garden grow!

## Did You See It?

dirt

food

plants

## Index